Peer Coaching Practice for Managers

An Executive Education Companion

PROF. KONSTANTIN KOROTOV, PhD

ISBN: 1491247037
ISBN-13: 978-1491247037

DEDICATION

This publication is dedicated to all those busy modern executives who find the time and energy to learn how to be helpful to their colleagues and subordinates. Good luck in becoming a great peer coach!

CONTENTS

	Acknowledgments	i
1	How to use this book	1
2	A few conceptual points	4
3	Minimum skills required from a peer coach	9
4	The simplest model to start peer coaching immediately	11
5	A sample peer coaching conversation	15
6	Peer coaching in a group setting	22
7	Practicing peer coaching with cases	25
8	Practice case: EMBA candidate	27
9	Practice case: Expatriate destination	30
10	Practice case: Family planning considerations	33
11	Practice case: Taking over a losing department	37
12	Practice case: Preparing for a difficult conversation	40

13 Practice case: Learning to delegate 44

14 Practice case: Am I a quota woman? 48

15 Practice case: Do I have a chance? 52

16 Practice case: Advice before moving to the West 56

17 Practice case: Bad presentations, bad 360 feedback 60

18 Practice case: Should I ask for more rewards? 64

19 Practice case: It's just too much 67

20 Practice case: Do I live up to my values? 70

21 Practice case: Following up on an action plan 74

22 Jump starting a coaching session in a Coachee role 78

23 Preparing for you peer coaching session in advance 80

24 Action plan 83

25 Your personal chapter 86

26 References 91

ACKNOWLEDGMENTS

I would like to acknowledge my participants in executive education programs all over the world and my former EMBA and MBA students for contribution of their personal stories and accounts of coaching and peer coaching experiences that formed the initial foundation of exercises and examples used in this book.

1 HOW TO USE THIS BOOK

This book was created to support participants in Executive Education, Executive MBA, and full-time MBA programs in developing and deepening their peer coaching skills. It was designed to serve the dual purpose of (1) being a set of course materials for discussion of the topic of peer coaching in executive education and (2) serving as a reference for those who act as peer coaches to their colleagues, fellow executive education participants, classmates, or friends.

The purpose of this book is to support the PRACTICE of peer coaching rather than to engage in a debate about the (still undeveloped) THEORY underlying the peer coaching processes and outcomes. For a deeper theoretical exploration of the topic of coaching and peer coaching the user can refer to publications mentioned in the references section, including some of the academic publications of the author.

The book is designed to be complemented by the reader's (or user's) own notes taken during an executive education program or working independently. Some space is dedicated for such a purpose throughout the book.

There is no need to read the whole book. If you are using it as part of a course, your instructor will refer you to the parts of this publication that are relevant for your program. You may be invited to use one or two chapters, cases, or exercises from this book. You may also be invited to use some of the chapters for your advance preparation for a course or a program, or for your post-course individual work. However, if at certain moment in your career or life you get interested in learning more about peer coaching, you may want to look through this book or challenge yourself with some of the exercises or cases.

This book may be recommended to those who toy with the idea of becoming a professional executive coach. While becoming a (decent) professional coach is a rather lengthy and demanding process, practicing peer coaching may be a good way of exploring the extent to which you like helping others and consider this as a potential career option. The practice cases from this book can be used for coaching training programs as well.

The book starts with a short conceptual Chapter 2 that provides some working concepts related to the practice of peer coaching. Acknowledging a variety of issues and discussions associated with the practice of peer coaching, it is important to underline the impossibility of addressing them fully in this publication.

Chapter 3 refers to peer coaching as meaningful conversation and describes the minimum skill required, namely that of active listening.

Chapter 4 describes a model that participants can start using immediately to practice peer coaching. This chapter can be used as a job aid or a support tool for acting as peer coach in an executive education course or in a work setting.

Chapter 5 presents a transcript of a sample peer coaching conversation for purposes of analysis in class or individual preparation.

Chapter 6 offers an algorithm for conducting a group peer coaching session. It can be used during an executive program as a guide for practicing peer coaching in a group. This chapter can be helpful for self-organized peer coaching groups.

Chapter 7 explains how to use practice cases presented further in the book as exercises in peer coaching.

Chapters 8 – 21 are examples of cases from peer coaching situations. They can be used for analysis in class or individual preparation of participants.

Chapter 22 can be used to make a quick preparation for a peer coaching session in the context of an executive education program. This chapter will be helpful when participants can't prepare for a peer coaching exercise in advance.

Chapter 23 offers a template that can be used for advanced preparation for peer coaching sessions.

Chapter 24 deals with making action plans and commitments on the basis of peer coaching exercises. It contains a template of a "Letter to myself" that can be collected in a sealed self-addressed envelope at the end of the course and mailed to participants a few weeks later to remind them about their action plans and commitments.

Chapter 25 is creative space provided for participants' own notes and observations taken during an executive education program or while working with this book.

Chapter 26 is a reference section.

YOUR NOTES:

2 A FEW CONCEPTUAL POINTS

A peer coaching situation is **a learning situation**, in which both, the Coachee and the Peer Coach (both of whom are practicing managers) will, hopefully, discover something about the Issue that the Coachee is facing, about the process of exploring the issue, about each other, and, last but not least, about oneself . This is an adult learning situation, and, unlike in many other learning situations, it is particularly important that there is a (conscious or unconscious) decision made by the involved adults in favor of making use of this learning opportunity (see, for example, Pätzold, 2011).

It is important to understand that adults bring into this type of learning situation their own well established picture of the world, perception of the coaching Issues at hand, and their own relationships with those Issues. In bringing a parallel from adult education theories, we can adapt a model of the so called "didactic triangle" of Arnold & Pätzold (2007) to the situation of peer coaching. In the adaptation of the "didactic triangle" model we can identify three elements: (1) the Coachee, (2) the Issue that the coachee needs or wants to discuss, and (3) the Peer Coach. The Peer coach takes the role of the moderator in the relationship between the Coachee and his or her Issue. It is still the Coachee who is in charge. The Issue remains her or his, and so does the relationship with it. However, the Peer Coach is invited (as we assume her or his voluntary involvement) by the Coachee to help her or him explore the nature of this relationship (Coachee – Issue) and, possibly, challenge it, reinforce it, or change it.

The relationship between the Coachee and her or his Issue exists within the framework of a socio-cultural context, i.e. other individuals, as well as habits, beliefs, interests, fears, anxieties, and hopes belonging to the world and situation in which the Coachee is embedded (for a discussion of the socio-cultural context in learning see, for example, Pätzold, 2011.). This socio-cultural concept influences the way the Coachee relates to his or her Issue. The Peer Coach (hopefully) coming from outside of this socio-cultural concept, but still able to understand it, may be a good resource for discovering alternative ways of relating to the Issue faced by the Coachee. As a result, the Coachee may be able to develop a broader repertoire of possible ways to manage relationship with his or her Issue, and, hopefully, make a better 'educated choice' related to one's behavior, career, communication, etc.

Making an educated choice at the end of the day means selecting a course of actions or adapting an attitude towards an Issue of importance to the Coachee based on a personal responsibility of the manager with acceptance of the positive results and, potentially, negative consequences of this choice. Ultimately, peer coaching is one of the ways by which a manager can be supported in making choices and feeling positive about her or his own agency, i.e. perceived ability to control the world around her or him.

Inevitably, in any case of a triangle (such as the Coachee, Peer Coach, and Issue), there is a dynamic of possible relationship between the Peer Coach and the Issue. The Peer Coach comes to the learning situation from her or his own socio-cultural situation, and she or he may have an established relationship with the Issue. It may not necessarily be the same instance of the Iissue, but the general archetype thereof. For example, the Issue faced by the Coachee may be the need to discipline a subordinate that fails to meet the Coachee's expectations, and the Peer Coach may have a well-developed relationship with the Issue of poor performance of subordinates in general. This well-developed relationship on the part of the Peer Coach may come in handy when and if the Coachee needs specific advice or script of how to deliver the message of her or his dissatisfaction with the performance of a subordinate. It can, however, be detrimental to the learning of the Coachee, if she or he needs to explore how the non-performance developed in a particular case, and what can be her or his own role in allowing or even causing this non-performance on the part of the subordinate.

While the discussion of the possible causes and consequences of the potential clashes between the type of relationships established with the Issue (or its various representations) on the part of the Coachee and Peer Coach is utterly fascinating, it is beyond the limits and purpose of this material. Suffice is to say that both the Coachee and the Peer Coach need to be aware of the influence their socio-cultural contexts and their own relationships with the Issue may have on the way the latter is viewed. The Peer Coach should, to the extent possible, notice and acknowledge the influence of her or his context and ways of relating to the Issue on the coaching discussion. At times she or he should make a conscientious attempt to suppress the expression of their well-established relationship to the Issue from directly affecting the coaching conversation. This is best done by first letting the Coachee to do most of the talking and asking her or him questions that would allow the latter to explore her or his own relationship with the Issue. On the other hand, the Coachee may be better off by letting her- or himself inquire at the end of their personal exploration what alternative relationship with the archetypical Issue may exist there, as represented by the Peer Coach's situation.

Unlike in a situation of professional executive coaching (where coaching refers to a service provided by a trained professional for a fee), peer coaching is explicitly a mutual learning opportunity whereby both executives involved (the Coachee and the Peer Coach) have a chance to learn about a variety of relationship that may exist between a human being and her or his Issue. Therefore, it has to be very clear from the very beginning of the peer coaching relationship that this is about learning and exploring, rather than necessarily finding (quick) solutions. As a minimum, the Coachee should leave the peer coaching session with curiosity about her or his relationship to the Issue, and the Peer Coach should be able to have a similar outcome regarding her or his respective relationship to the (potential) Issue. At the end of the day, Peer Coaching may be viewed as learning based on the social exchange of equally competent partners who enable each other to reach new levels of development. This definition is adapted from a view about what learning is by Rehr & Gruber (2007) as represented in Pätzold (2011: 29). For discussion of application of peer coaching to executive education please refer to Korotov (2008).

Any interaction between human beings, including that of a learning nature, is potentially subject to a variety of psychodynamic influences. This important and exciting field is a subject of multiple studies and requires a lengthy explanation and exploration. However, it is important to draw the attention of the Peer Coach and the Coachee to at least the phenomena of "transference" and "counter-transference" that can happen in the process of peer coaching. "Transference encompasses both the belief and the process that feelings and attitudes connected with the past are experienced and re-enacted in the present relationships." (Coren, 1997: 46). It is very helpful to recognize this psychological mix-up of the time and place (e.g.

the Coachee subconsciously expecting from the Peer Coach playing of the role of a supportive older brother or getting into the game of outsmarting the latter in a revival of relationship with a competitive sister).

A related concept is that of counter-transference, whereby the Peer Coach is reviving a situation of relationship with someone from her or his past (e.g. a former subordinate who refuses to listen to the Peer Coach's ideas or suggestions). Asking oneself "Does this conversation remind me of similar experiences in my life?" and then bringing this to the open may require a certain discipline, level of psychological astuteness, and some degree of courage. It can happen that a certain experience with peer coaching may be required before a person can recognize the traces of transference or counter-transference in her or his peer coaching interactions. Once encounter with countertransference can also become clear in a professional coaching or supervision session where an executive wants to reflect on her or his peer coaching experience. It should be noted that professional executive coaches are expected to undergo professional supervision where they can work with their own ability to detect and use countertransference productively (as a way of informing themselves by noticing their own feelings about what may be going in the Coachee during the conversation).

Psychological safety is a critical concept in peer coaching. The participants in the process should feel comfortable expressing their stories, exposing their relationship to their Issues, and developing scenarios and discussing their consequences. An open discussion is only possible when the parties involved know that whatever is being discussed is not going to be used to their detriment (objective or psychological), such as negative work-related consequences, feelings of guilt or shame, being ridiculed, or having to explain and defend themselves vis-à-vis third parties. The process has to be mutual for the Peer Coach and the Coachee.

When the Peer Coach cares about the manager who is in the Coachee position, but is not personally affected by the eventual choices made by the latter, he or she can be most helpful and productive. Being personally disinterested in the effects of the outcomes of the Coachee's decisions frees the Peer Coach from the risks associated with envy, jealousy, rivalry, feeling of own incompetence or lack of luck, etc. The Peer Coach should recognize the situations where she or he may become "an interested party" (which can be at the psychological well-being level, rather than at the level of material interest or career rivalry) and then discuss the possible limitations of her or his involvement in the peer coaching situation.

It is equally important to make an official (albeit oral and informal) commitment of both parties to the confidentiality of the discussions held in the context of peer coaching.

YOUR NOTES:

3 MINIMUM SKILLS REQUIRED FROM A PEER COACH

People are not born as coaches or peer coaches. Being a decent Peer Coach requires some skills, but quite a lot of those should have been obtained by a manager through her or his previous training and career development. If not, than practicing to be a Peer Coach may come in handy for development of general management skills (as well as general human competencies).

In a nutshell, **peer coaching is a meaningful conversation**. Therefore, the Peer Coach should be a helpful conversation partner, making the discussion meaningful for the Coachee and her- or himself. The minimum skill required is that of **active listening**.

Active listening involves a conscientious attempt on the part of the Peer Coach to give the maximum of her or his attention to what the Coachee is saying. In particular, it means to be **mentally present** in the time and the situation of the physical conversation. This involves removing the distractors (such as smartphones, documents, newspapers, etc.), assuring the reasonable physical comfort (such as arranging the chairs allowing for a relaxed conversation), and minimizing the impact of other distractors (such as possible interruptions by other people). Maintaining reasonable eye contact and, if necessary, taking notes in order not to interrupt the Coachee when she or he is in the flow of a story are also elements of being mentally present.

Active listening also means **acknowledging** what the other person has said (even if the Peer Coach is in disagreement with the statement made), and checking for her or his own understanding of the statements. Most often this can be made in the form of **paraphrasing** or **summarizing** what the Coachee has just expressed. Acknowledgement and paraphrasing are necessary to show to the Coachee that the Peer Coach has listened to her or him, has heard her or him, and has understood her or him. Paraphrasing and sometimes repeating certain elements of what has been said is also a good way to encourage the Coachee to continue speaking and developing her or his story further. Summarizing can be useful to underline some of the important points expressed, and, if necessary, to bring the discussion back to the point, in case the conversation wanders away from its course.

Another important element of active listening is **reflecting the perceived feelings** of the Coachee by the Peer Coach. The latter can acknowledge what, based on her or his interpretation of the Coachee's words, might be taking place in the mind and heart of the speaker.

Last but not least, active listening involves **asking questions** with the purposes of clarification, probing, development of hypotheses, and asking for commitment. In general, asking open questions is more productive than asking closed questions.

Active listening is not about arguing with the person but rather about learning how the Coachee is related to her or his Issue. It may require some discipline on the part of the Peer Coach to avoid a temptation of "being right" and instead focusing on a learning opportunity, even if the Peer Coach has a strong view on what the Coachee is talking about.

If you are using this book in a course, your instructor is likely to provide you with additional information and exercises on practicing active listening, and if you are practicing Peer Coaching for the first time, you may want to ask for feedback about your use of active listening from your Peer Coachee or observers involved in exercises.

YOUR NOTES:

4 THE SIMPLEST MODEL TO START PEER COACHING IMMEDIATELY

There are multiple models of running a coaching conversation that can be applied to Peer Coaching. For examples of a variety of models the reader can refer to Allamby (2006). However, since the focus of this publication is the practice of peer coaching, this chapter provides a simplified version of one of the most popular coaching models, namely the GROW model. This model is often associated with the name of John Whitmore who published a version of it in 1992. This model has been picked up and expanded and enhanced by many practitioners and authors.

In a nutshell, the acronym GROW reflects what coaches are expected to do: help their clients grow professionally and personally. Each of the letters in the acronym stands for a stage in a coaching conversation which allows to explore and discover the Coachee's relationship with her or his Issue.

The GROW model suggests that in a coaching session a Peer Coach can steer the Coachee through the following conversation stages:

- determining the **Goal** of the Coachee's effort;
- assessing the current **Reality** faced by the Coachee (as related to her or his Goal);
- identifying and analysing **Options** (and resources) available to the Coachee in reaching her or his goal; and
- supporting the **Will** of the Coachee to work on the options and use the resources identified.

The author's experience suggests that participants in Executive Education, EMBA, and MBA programs can start quite successful coaching conversations with the help of this tool even if they have never experienced coaching or peer coaching before.

Some suggested questions for your session that follows the GROW model are provided below. These questions are partly adapted versions of questions suggested by Whitmore (2002) and Landsberg (1997), and partly suggestions based on the experience of peer coaching within executive education.

Goal:

- What would you like to take as an outcome of today's discussion?
- How do you see my role in helping you with your objectives?
- What are you trying to achieve?
- What form of outcome are you seeking from engaging in this project or activity?
- How determined are you in pursuing this goal? What can stop you from pursuing it?
- In the long term what is your personal goal related to this project? What is the time frame?
- In working towards your goal, what intermediate steps can you identify, with their time frames?

Reality:

- What is the present situation in this field/area/project?
- What are the chances of success of your project as it stands now?
- What and how great is your concern about it?
- Who is affected by this project's taking place or not taking place other than you?
- Who is informed about your desire to implement this idea/start this project?
- How much control do you personally have over the outcome?
- Who else has some control over it and how much?
- What action steps have you taken on it so far?
- What stopped you from doing more?
- What obstacles will need to be overcome on the way?

- What may be some of your own, personal resistances or obstacles that you have to overcome in order to achieve the desired outcomes?
- What, if any, internal obstacles or personal resistances of other people do you have to take into account when planning your actions?
- What resources (e.g. skill, time, enthusiasm, money, support, etc.) do you already have?
- What other resources will you need? Where could you get them from?

Options:

- What are other different ways in which you could approach this issue? What are alternatives to the project you have in mind?
- Make a list of all the alternatives, large or small, complete and partial solutions.
- What else could you do?
- What would you do if you had more time, a larger budget or if you were the boss?
- What would you do if you could start again with a clean sheet, with a new team?
- Would you like to hear a suggestion from me?
- What are the advantages and disadvantages of each of these in turn?
- Which would give the best result?
- Which of these solutions appeals to you most, of feels best to you?
- Which of these options would give you the most satisfaction?

Will:

- Which option or options do you find most promising?
- To what extent does this meet all or most of your objectives?
- What are your criteria and measurements for success for the project? For your personal involvement in this project?
- What are the specific action steps? When precisely are you going to start and finish each action step?
- What will be your quick wins?
- How are you going to inform others about your quick wins?

- What could arise to hinder you in taking these steps or meeting the goal?
- What personal resistance do you have, if any, to taking these steps?
- What will you do to eliminate or soften external and internal resistance factors?
- Who needs to know about your plans?
- What support do you need and from whom?
- What will you do to obtain that support and when?
- Is there anything else you want to talk about now or are we finished?
- How do you want to follow up on this conversation?

YOUR NOTES:

5 A SAMPLE PEER COACHING CONVERSATION

This is a script of a peer coaching conversation between John (a Peer Coachee) and Peter (a Peer Coach). John and Peter met previously in the same Executive MBA program. The current coaching conversation takes places at an Alumni meeting several years after graduation from their program.

John: Well, Peter, thanks for giving me an opportunity to discuss with you the issue that I am facing right now. I am really new in my role, and I don't yet have the kind of relationships with the people around me at my new workplace that would allow me to be frank and open in discussing my challenges. I remember the atmosphere of our coaching sessions during our EMBA program, so I am looking forward to picking your brain and experience for some help again.

Peter: No problem, John. I think I learned a lot during our coaching sessions, and I am looking forward to the experience again. So, what would you like to achieve in our coaching session today?

John: I would like to talk to you about my current situation and see if what I am doing is right. I need a fresh look at my problems and the way I handle them. And, maybe, you could suggest some solutions to me.

Peter: As you remember, they always told us in the EMBA program that finding solutions remains the responsibility of the Coachee, haven't they? Anyway, let's start with the description of the situation you are facing right now.

John: OK, as you know, two months ago I started in a new position as head of internal consulting at Bearlingo Assurances, a large insurance company. I moved there from internal consulting at XYZ. As you know, XYZ is a huge industrial conglomerate, and it has had internal consulting as part of its operations for more than twenty-five years by now. At Bearlingo Assurances, this is a completely new story. They organized a small department the role of which was defined to help streamline business processes about two-and-a-half years ago. They have been struggling with it ever since. Initially, they hired a former large consulting powerhouse person to set up the department who immediately brought in a lot of McKinsey-type people. They instantly rolled up their sleeves and set down to identifying the company's issues and started going around interviewing people, asking for all sorts of data, and producing PowerPoint slides. They felt they knew what they were doing, but they failed to realize that unlike staff from a big consultancy they couldn't walk away after presenting their slides. The company was expecting them to be involved in the implementation part, and that's where these people realized that there was a lot of resistance to their ideas and plans, that nobody was going to dedicate energy and effort, to say nothing of real budgets, for getting things accomplished according to their plans. To cut a long story short, the head of the department left, and so did a few internal consultants. When they brought me in, they thought that my in-house consulting experience with XYZ would make me a better fit than someone who walks in directly from a strategy consulting firm. After my EMBA I found this to be an attractive opportunity, as within XYZ the hierarchy is so heavy that I wouldn't be able to run the whole show for years, and here I could start with a my own shop and quite some freedom to decide what I should do. The job opportunity sounded very exciting, and I thought that I could do things right. You might remember that during the EMBA I often complained about how bureaucratic and inflexible the consulting part of XYZ was, and that I didn't feel comfortable in an environment that had lost its flexibility and speed. So a month ago I started at Bearlingo Assurances.

Peter: It sounds like you were very excited to take the job because it gave you a chance to be the boss and run your own show, although the function is smaller than what you are accustomed to. And, it sounds like you want to make a difference.

John: Correct. I joined full of excitement, and I still am very excited about this job. What happened is that with the departure of a few employees, I am currently left with a much smaller group than what is required in terms of expectations that the company has for our work. The people who stayed are a bit frustrated with the way they are viewed by the rest of the organization. The company seems to be disappointed with the previous experience with the consulting group, and, as a result, it doesn't take the group seriously.

Peter: I hear at least three issues here. The first one is about the headcount. You say that you don't have enough people. The second issue is related to the morale of the team. I hear that people are frustrated. The third one is about the way the organization treats your team. You say that they don't take it seriously. Which of the issues, do you think, you need to work most energetically on?

John: Well, it sounds like the third one is the real issue here. If the organization doesn't take us seriously, there is no point in trying to boost up morale or looking for good people elsewhere. I guess you are going to suggest that we should work on this one.

Peter: I think we should work on whatever is important to you.

John: Right. I think the way the internal consulting department is currently treated at Bearlingo Assurances is something that keeps me awake at night. I really need to make sure that we are taken seriously, only then I will be able to develop a well-functioning internal consulting function.

Peter: What, in an ideal case, would this "being taken seriously" mean for you and your department?

John: I guess it would mean that people consider me and my function to be a valuable trusted advisor who can contribute to achievement of the organizational goals by offering the knowledge and the tools that we as a team have to analyze the situation, develop a course of action, and support the process of implementation.

Peter: That sounds almost like a mission statement for your function.

John: You are right. I have been thinking about this formulation of our *raison d'etre* for some time. And I am pretty determined in making this endeavor a success, as I wouldn't have left my comfortable position at XYZ if I didn't want to make a difference.

Peter: And what does the situation look like right now? What makes you think that the organization doesn't take your function seriously?

John: To give you an example, I should quote a project that was started before I came on board. The project involved quite a lot of analytical work, but as the team was ready to present it during virtually my first week on the job, it became known that an almost exactly the same task was given to an external consulting company, and they were presenting to the Board. We hadn't even been told that an external company would be involved in this project.

Peter: And what makes you say that they don't take you seriously? You've mentioned that you wanted to be taken seriously by Bearlingo Assurancess.

John: I guess they could have told me when I started that there was this parallel work being done by an external consultancy. That really drove me crazy to find out about this situation.

Peter: And even if they did, would this have changed anything related to the project or your decision to join the company?

John: Hmmm. I guess not. The project was coming to an end at that moment. And I certainly wouldn't take this as a reason for not joining.

Peter: Are there any other signals that they don't take you seriously at Bearlingo Assurancess?

John: I don't have that much evidence, but it feels like something is going on and I might be missing the action. I mean being invited to important strategy meetings, or even having a serious conversation with a function leader or a market leader, maybe even informally.

Peter: So, if I hear you correctly, the sense that you are not being invited to important discussions makes you feel that you are not being valued personally.

John: I guess so. I think that my personal credibility could eventually contribute to the credibility of the whole team. I believe I need to work on it, because if they don't trust me, the "horns" effect that we studied in the Organizational Behavior course in our EMBA will eventually haunt the whole team. Hmmm. Peter, it looks like you are doing a good job as a peer coach. I think I realize that it could be my personal credibility with the organizational critical stakeholders that should be part of my immediate agenda.

Peter: Great to hear that you now know that the current reality, your personal credibility with the critical organizational stakeholders, is such that it is not supporting your goal, that of making your department a valuable part of the organization. It sounds like you have realized that you need to work on the way the organization perceives you. You know, the thing that comes to my mind is the discussion we had in our Organizational Behavior class on the dispositional trust, the trust that is not yet based on your achievements or keeping your promises, but rather on the psychological comfort that people have when they need to rely on you. Could it be that the fact that you come from outside not only Bearlingo Assurancess, but also from the outside of the insurance industry in general, makes you too different for people to accept you? Or, could it be that they simply don't know you enough?

John: Good that you remembered that Organizational Behavior course. When the prof told us that this stuff would probably be the most important for our professional future, I didn't really take him seriously. Now it looks like all of my problems are related to people issues. I think you are right in both of your hypotheses. I could be too different for people, and they may not know what to expect of me. And I think I haven't done enough to make it easier for them to know about me or my plans for the consulting department.

Peter: So?

John: I guess I need to start working with critical individuals in my organization. I need to identify key stakeholders and work on relationships with them.

Peter: And how could you go about that?

John: Well, I guess the first step is making the list of the critical stakeholders. I actually have that in the back of my head already. I believe I would start with those who have been the most critical of the department in the past to try to present myself and to find out what their concerns are. I should also ask some of my people who the most difficult people they have dealt with are and add those to my list as well.

Peter: Is there anyone else whom you should consult with regard to the list of the most critical stakeholders?

John: That would probably be my boss, the Senior VP for Strategy. I need to sit down with him to present the results of my "audit" of the departmental situation, and I think I can also use this as an opportunity to check with him the list of the most critical stakeholders. I could also ask him for help to get appointments with some of the senior people.

Peter: What else could you do?

John: I think I could also talk to my boss about a possibility to present the departmental vision to a broader audience.

Peter: Are you ready to do that?

John: Actually, it doesn't make sense, does it? I need to talk to people first to find out what their expectations of us are. No, I am not ready to present my departmental vision yet.

Peter: So, what will be the actionable steps now?

John: I will make a list of critical stakeholders with whom I need to talk individually. I think I will take a consulting approach, without calling it that way, and explore the expectations these individuals have of the consulting function within the organization. I will also use this as an opportunity to present myself and my expertise, and try to communicate my willingness to support them in working with their challenges.

Peter: And, I guess, as peer coach I need to ask you when you are going to do that?

John: I will start making the list this evening. I will talk to my people this week. I will talk to my boss next week. I think I will establish the first contacts in no more than two weeks.

Peter: And how will you keep yourself on track?

John: I think I will need to keep you informed about how I am doing, right? No worries, I will not bother you too much.

Peter: Actually, I am very interested how it goes. I find the question of establishing personal credibility to be very important, and, at times scary. I really want to learn from your experience.

John: Deal. Let's get in touch in about a month's time and see how it goes.

Peter: So, we are almost finished. How did it go for you?

John: This was very helpful, thank you. I started with seeing this whole new job and the situation with the team as a set of various issues and problems. Now I think I know that in my case establishing a personal credibility with key stakeholders will be critically important for my ability to deal with all the other issues involved. And some people still say that there is nothing personal in business. Don't believe them! And how was it for you, Peter, to run a coaching session with me?

Peter: I learned something myself. I recognize that I often fail into a situation where I expect people to treat me in a particular way without giving them enough information about me or my work that would actually allow them to treat me that way. I saw a few parallels to my current work situation, and I will want to discuss them with you after we have reviewed your progress next time. Maybe we should budget a bit more time for our next meeting so that you could coach me?

John: I will be happy to do so. I should also mention that I need to write to my Organizational Behavior professor and acknowledge that he was right when he said that we need to develop a network of people with whom we can talk when we need help.

YOUR NOTES:

6 PEER COACHING IN A GROUP SETTING

The pioneering work of bringing group peer coaching to executive education done by Prof. Manfred Kets de Vries and his colleagues at INSEAD and the continuation of this work at ESMT – European School of Management and Technology strongly support the belief in the power of the group in helping an individual explore her or his relationship with the Issue (challenge, opportunity, hope, fear, anxiety, etc.) at hand. For an in-depth discussion of group coaching please refer to Kets de Vries, Korotov, & Florent-Treacy (2007), Kets de Vries, Guillen, Korotov, & Florent-Treacy (2010), Kets de Vries (2011), Korotov, Florent-Treacy, Kets de Vries, & Bernhardt (2012).

While the group coaching work presupposes the presence and active involvement of a well-trained professional coach, in the situation of peer coaching a lot can be achieved even in the absence of a qualified professional in charge of the session. For the purposes of this book and the intended uses of it, peer coaching in a group setting is viewed as a learning opportunity suitable for a (small) group of motivated managers who want to deepen their understanding of managerial and human issues relevant for them and their peers.

The following tool suggested for use in group peer coaching has been experienced by the author in a variety of settings: conferences, executive education courses, supervision and para-supervision sessions, etc. It has been impossible so far to establish the exact authorship or the origin of the tool. Some of the most productive variations of the tool have been observed by the author at executive education courses at Harvard Kennedy School of Governance (the program of Ron Heifetz), at the INSEAD Global Leadership Center conferences, and at the ESMT Coaching

Colloquium and some of the ESMT executive course (e.g. designed by Ulf Schaefer).

The common idea behind all of those variations of the peer coaching model is that the collective mind and heart of the executives can be used productively to help the Coachee explore the relationship with his or her Issue. The group can also have accelerated learning by exploring the other people's reaction (and underlying relationship) with the Issue faced by the Coachee.

The tool below presupposes that there is at least a 60-minute time-slot available for each of the Coachees participating in the group peer coaching process. Some time is needed upfront for setting the group and establishing the ground rules. In some programs the time slots for group peer coaching may be spread across several different sessions or even different days.

Setting the group (before the actual work starts)

- Make sure that there is willingness of people to participate.
- Handle possible conflicts related to people working in the same organization (if any).
- Reiterate the understanding of the confidentiality of the discussions in the group.
- Remind each other about the need to listen actively.
- Make sure that the distracting factors are minimized (e.g. communication devices are turned off).
- Assign the time-keeper who is responsible for reminding the group about the stages of the process and the time available.

The Process of Peer Group Coaching:

Presentation of the Coachee's Story (Issue) – 15 minutes

- The Coachee briefly explains what she or he wants to achieve as a result of the discussion
- The Coachee presents her or his story (case) There should be a brief presentation of the current situation, plus an explanation of what the person wants to see as an ideal outcome. If she or he has already tried something, this needs to be explained as well. A brief summary of stakeholders' interests and conflicts can be helpful.

Clarification Questions – 10 minutes

- The Peer Coaches ask clarification questions in order to better understand the situation. The Coachee provides clarifying answers.

- The Peer Coaches refrain from offering their interpretations, views, explanation, hypotheses, advice, or suggestions. This is the time for getting necessary details only.

Collective Exploration – 20 minutes

- The Coachee turns away from the group so that she or he doesn't see the other participants but can still hear them well. The Coachee listens without reacting or responding, but taking notes of what she or he hears.
- The Peer Coaches take turns to express and explore their own reactions, association, feelings, thoughts, ideas. They don't ask the Coachee for reaction.
- Peer coaches can build on commentaries made by others. It is important, however, that everyone has had a chance to express her or his reaction.

Clarifications from the Coachee – 5 minutes

- The Coachee asks clarifying questions, if any.

Summary and Action Plan by the Coachee – 5 minutes

- The Coachee summarizes the most striking points (something that has 'hit' or surprised her or him) from the discussion.
- The coachee explains what his or he next steps (actions) will be.

Learning points – 5 minutes

- Each of the participants shares what her or his learning points from this experience are.
- The Coachee concludes with her or his learning points.

YOUR NOTES:

7 PRACTICING PEER COACHING WITH CASES

In the following chapters you will find a selection of cases that present stories of managers who look for peer coaching as an opportunity to learn how to handle their Issues. While all of these cases have a real background, their protagonists have been made unidentifiable in order to protect the identity of the people who have volunteered to share them. Names, ages, types of industries, countries of origin, location, and other pieces of information have been modified.

Cases serve as material for reflection and discussion, not as expressions of right or wrong behaviors or actions on the part of the managers. The idea is to present realistic scenarios that would allow the reader (course participant) to contemplate her or his possible way of helping the Coachee explore the relationship with her or his Issue in the role of a Peer Coach.

The cases can also serve a fruitful start for the Peer Coach's own reflection on her or his management practices and an opportunity to reflect on her or his own Issues.

Ideally, a case from the selection below should be read individually. Then the Peer Coach should think about the questions related to the case. It is helpful to jot down the thoughts in the space provided after each question. The participants can then compare their own answers to the questions with colleagues participating in a Peer Coaching program. This can create an opportunity to compare approaches to the Issue and explore one's own relationship with it.

For the purposes of practicing peer coaching, some cases can be turned into role plays where one person plays the role of the Coachee, the other –

of the Peer Coach, and a third person – the role of an observer. The observer watches the process, take notes, and then provide feedback to the Peer Coach in terms of the use by the latter of the minimum skills required (e.g. active listening) and a model/models that are used in the course.

The questions that are to be considered after reading the case are:

- What is my first reaction to the story presented?
- What seems to be the Issue here?
- What do I need to find out in the discussion with the Coachee in order to be of help to him or her?
- Do I have a story from my experience that is related to this case and that I could (eventually) share with the Coachee?
- Do I experience any additional thoughts or feelings?

YOUR NOTES:

8 PRACTICE CASE: EMBA CANDIDATE

Robert is a 37 year-old manager at a large financial services institution. He feels he is doing very well career-wise, enjoys a constantly growing set of responsibilities given to him, and keeps looking for new challenges. He believes he spends more time and energy at work than an average person in similar positions, and he thinks that this is the right thing to do in order to secure a steady career progress. Besides, it's great fun!

Robert is married to a 35 year-old Svenja, who works for a large utilities company and enjoys her job and career progress very much, despite the demanding nature of her position. Svenja has an MBA from a US business school which she got at the age of 28. Both Svenja and Robert try to spend whatever little of the free time they have outdoors together: they go bouldering, hiking, and sailing in summer, and they ski and snowboard in winter.

Friday last week Pablo, Robert's boss, asked him to stop by his office for a quick chat. He then told Robert that he had just been called by the HR department and told about a possibility to nominate a candidate for an Executive MBA program sponsored by the company. The HR, according to Robert's boss, made it clear that the company sponsored very few people pursuing an EMBA as, despite the fact that the CEO supported the idea, it was not totally clear how this investment in additional education of a few people would benefit the company as a whole. They asked Pablo to think about a person who, if successful in pursuing the EMBA, would be able to put the newly acquired knowledge and skills to work and would demonstrate through professional achievements and career progress that the investment was worthwhile.

Pablo mentioned that he was pleased that the HR thought about his division when exploring where to get candidates for the EMBA program. Pablo (who doesn't have an MBA himself) said that Robert was the only candidate he had in mind and that he wanted to nominate him. The HR needed to hear from Robert's boss within a week, as they were already late with the nominations, approvals, and application procedures. Pablo gave Robert the name of the contact person in HR and said that he needed to hear from Robert by the middle of the week.

Robert contacted the HR and found out about the name of the school offering the EMBA (he has never heard of this institution before), the duration of the program (18 months), and a list of requirements for applying. The program would actually start in four months from now, and, if Robert were nominated, he would need to go through admission tests and interviews pretty soon.

Back home Robert told Svenja about this proposition. He felt, on the one hand, flattered by the offer but, on the other hand, was a bit unclear about what this opportunity would require from him. Svenja had always referred to her experience in a full-time two year MBA program as one of the best times in her life, but now she seemed a bit more reserved. She said that MBA required a lot of work and time, and she couldn't really picture how Robert would combine it with his busy professional and personal schedule.

Checking his emails one last time before going to bed, Robert finds a message from the HR person he has been in contact with mentioning the name and email address of a person who happens to have an EMBA from the program for which Robert might be nominated. The HR person has already spoken to that individual and he is happy to meet for lunch on the next day, if Robert is available. Robert immediately sends a confirmation to the person who is eager to talk to him and a thank you to the HR contact.

CASE REFLECTION QUESTIONS:

What is my first reaction to the story presented?

____

____

____

____

____

____

What seems to be the Issue here?

____
____
____
____
____
____

What do I need to find out in the discussion with the Coachee in order to be of help to him or her?

____
____
____
____
____
____

Do I have a story from my experience that is related to this case and that I could (eventually) share with the Coachee?

____
____
____
____
____
____

Do I experience any additional thoughts or feelings?

____
____
____
____
____
____

YOUR NOTES:

9 PRACTICE CASE: EXPATRIATE DESTINATION

Martin is a 35-year-old financial professional. Working for a large bank, he has built a career starting with an apprenticeship program and completing his bachelor's degree in parallel. He enjoys his work, and feels appreciated by his organization. He is married to a 36-years-old Roxanna, a medical doctor working in a large public hospital. They have two children, three and five years old.

About 18 months ago Martin participated in an Assessment Center for high potential managers and completed a series of career-planning discussions with a group of people, involving his boss and HR professionals. It has become clear from those discussions that Martin meets the profile of high potential managers the company is looking for. The only thing that is missing in Martin's portfolio of skills and experiences is an expatriate assignment.

Martin has declined previous opportunities for an overseas mission because of personal reasons. Once an assignment was offered when his wife was still in the process of an important part of her medical doctor's training and examinations, and Martin decided to wait until she was done with those. The other assignment was turned down when Martin and Roxanna were expecting their second child and doctors suspected some possible complications with the baby's health. Luckily, the child was born healthy.

After the Assessment Center and career discussions, Martin sat down to talk to Roxanna, and they both agreed that he had to make himself available for an overseas mission. Martin clearly indicated this intent to his superior and ticked "ready for an overseas mission" box in his on-line career development plan.

Martin has received a series of signals from his boss that an interesting overseas task for Martin is in the making. Quite a few new developments in the bank's operations in the United States suggested that there would be a few interesting opportunities there. The boss has asked a couple of times if Martin liked American food and was ready to live in a big city. He was invited a couple of times to attend big meetings where the future of the US operations of the bank was on the agenda. He was quite sure that they would be heading across the Atlantic pretty soon.

Roxanna knew that she would be unlikely to be able to work in the US as a medical doctor due to educational system differences and due to the fact that the childcare arrangements might be complicated, but she found a couple of interesting opportunities to engage in further specialized coursework with research-oriented medical schools. She could later use that as part of her planned PhD in medical research. Roxanna even looked at the list of required documentation necessary to apply for courses and started a long process of collecting transcripts and other paperwork.

Martin was not surprised when his boss called him one morning and told him to start packing for a move across the Atlantic. The destination, however, turned out to be quite different. Instead of the US, the bank was offering him an opportunity in Brazil. Brazil, a booming business destination, was definitively not an easy place for a family with two small kids. Besides, Roxanna's plans, which, actually, made her feel very excited, now needed a serious correction. The boss, however, told Martin that Brazil would be a significantly more interesting chance for his future career than any kind of comparable assignment anywhere else in the world. The bank's CEO declared that market to be a top priority for the company.

Martin has been postponing the conversation with his wife for several days. The time, however, is running out. He needs to go into the nitty-gritty discussions of the technical terms of his relocation no later than next week. It is an unwritten policy in his organization that when you go in this type of discussions, you have agreed to the assignment in principle.

CASE REFLECTION QUESTIONS:

What is my first reaction to the story presented?

____

____

____

What seems to be the Issue here?

What do I need to find out in the discussion with the Coachee in order to be of help to him or her?

Do I have a story from my experience that is related to this case and that I could (eventually) share with the Coachee?

Do I experience any additional thoughts or feelings?

YOUR NOTES:

10 PRACTICE CASE: FAMILY PLANNING CONSIDERATIONS

Maureen is a 38 year-old Research and Development manager at a large pharmaceutical. She is a living example of a great career. When she was done with her PhD in Biological Chemistry at the age of 26, she took a job with one of the best academic research laboratories and was then headhunted for a research position at a prestigious pharmaceutical company. She was quickly put on a 'young-talent' program which meant a lot of training and development opportunities, mentoring by senior people in the organization, high visibility of the assignments, and a lot of support from the organization.

As a result of the program, Maureen quickly realized that she enjoyed the managerial aspects of the R&D business as much, and even more, as she enjoyed the laboratory work. She did a number of multinational projects and spent two years in developing a new research center her company had just established in China, which was a great success for the company and a lot of fun for Maureen.

Five years ago Maureen married Gregg, who is two years her senior, an IT professional working for a large NGO. Mary and Gregg share a lot of hobbies and, importantly, values. They both believe in behaving towards others the way you want others to behave towards you. They both acknowledge how good their employers are treating them and are ready to respond in kind.

When doing her EMBA (again, sponsored and fully supported by the company), Maureen was often astonished by the stories her classmates told about their evil bosses, unreasonable demands from the company, or ridiculous roadblocks on trying to get anything done in organizations that bore some of the best-known brand names in their industries. Maureen thought that she must have been extremely lucky with the way her organization and bosses treated her. She was paid very well, but there was much more to it. She once even told her classmates how her boss offered her to make a special arrangement with flexible working hours for Maureen when she had told her that her elderly father was developing an Alzheimer and needed a lot of attention and special care. Maureen was very touched by this offer, although she didn't make use of it, as a suitable assisted living arrangement was found, and a combination of the father's insurance and Maureen's own financial contribution (while unbearable for most people, still affordable to Maureen) allowed her to feel good about her father and continue to do her job.

At a romantic dinner celebrating Gregg's 40th birthday, he tells Maureen that he thinks it's time they had kids. Gregg's parents keep complaining about getting old and not having grandchildren. While jokingly dismissing their attempt to influence Gregg and Maureen's life, Gregg makes it clear that he is ready to be a father. Maureen is really glad that they have this conversation, because she has started developing a feeling that, despite the fact that she always imagined herself as a mother, she has been postponing important decisions, with pressing career issues being the most frequent excuse. They talk long, sipping Veuve Cliquot, feeling determined about the next important step in their life together.

There is unexpected news back at work. Claire, Maureen's boss, walks in her office with a big smile. She has good news. Maureen is being promoted to a new and exciting position of the head of a laboratory network spanning several countries (including the research center Maureen developed in China). This is really big! Maureen is very happy, because she had pushed for this network approach to R&D in her company since her Executive MBA practice project and Master Thesis times! It is finally being implemented (and her boss acknowledges that it is thanks to her, Maureen's ideas and efforts). Claire is very excited. She acknowledges that it will be a lot of work, a lot of travel across several continents, and, probably, lots of sleepless nights and busy weekends, at least for the first two or three years. She is also very confident that Maureen has the right competencies, attitude, and commitment to the organization. She concludes: "I am glad that the company made a lot of investment in you, Maureen! I always knew that we would get a great payoff some day!"

Driving home that afternoon, Maureen tries to reconcile what they agreed upon with Gregg, their common dream about becoming parents, and what will be required of her, as she moves into a new job, in fact, her professional dream for the past several years. Would she betray the company, the people that invested in her, and the dream she has had about R&D network? Should she and Gregg postpone their family planning efforts?

CASE REFLECTION QUESTIONS:

What is my first reaction to the story presented?

____
____
____
____
____
____

What seems to be the Issue here?

____
____
____
____
____
____

What do I need to find out in the discussion with the Coachee in order to be of help to him or her?

____
____
____
____
____
____

Do I have a story from my experience that is related to this case and that I could (eventually) share with the Coachee?

____
____
____
____
____
____

Do I experience any additional thoughts or feelings?

YOUR NOTES:

11 PRACTICE CASE: TAKING OVER A LOSING DEPARTMENT

Marcus is a 35-year-old former consultant. Having reached a Senior Manager level in a large consulting company, he decided to move into "the real world" and prove to himself (as well as to some of his close friends who have always made fun of him saying that "those who can't, consult") that he actually could make a difference in executing good ideas that he could easily generate for companies in need of advice. Besides, the prospects of becoming a partner in his previous company were getting thinner and thinner due to a challenging market situation and loss of the company's competitive advantage caused, in the opinion of Marcus, by political struggles among senior partners.

A call from a headhunter came in handy. The job was with a large global corporation with a great reputation. The job title was "Head of Global HR Shared Services" and the reporting line was directly to the Senior VP Human Resources. The headhunter underlined that the fact that Marcus had worked on a number of shared services projects with global companies in his consulting role was a huge advantage for his candidacy, although he had never had a pure HR background in his CV. The meetings with the company went very well. Marcus was told that the HR Shared Services had been on the company's agenda for a while, that two of the previous heads of HR Global Shared Services were asked to leave due to lack of satisfactory results, and that the Board was losing patience. The recently hired Senior VP for HR made it clear that her own success would be partially measured on the situation with the Global HR Shared Services, and that she needed someone who would be able to fix the situation as quickly as possible.

Marcus met with a couple of people from the team who told him about the challenges they experienced in their work caused, in their opinion, by complete lack of support from anyone in the organization. Some people even mentioned that colleagues were making jokes about the HR Shared Services being a place where the company would send all of its most useless people. Marcus didn't really like the team members he had a chance to speak to, but he was impressed by the Senior VP for HR and a couple of other HR managers, particularly the head of Learning and Development, who, as it turned out, had come from the same consulting company as Marcus. The compensation package was quite attractive. Marcus decided to take the challenge.

The first week on the job was spent trying to figure out the current status of the HR Shared Services. Marcus was reviewing the internal documents, talking to team members, and reading emails that started pouring on the second day of his job tenure with complaints from people in various countries who couldn't get the services they needed. The first week ended with an understanding that people on the team he had managed to talk to were frustrated, demotivated, and, probably, not fully qualified to do their job properly. The tone of emails with complaints suggested that users of the shared services were utterly frustrated. A couple of issues that started before his arrival were currently somewhere high in the hierarchy, as they had been escalated to the top and were now on the radar screen of the senior leadership in the organization. The first week was over. Marcus wondered what he should be doing next Monday.

CASE REFLECTION QUESTIONS:

What is my first reaction to the story presented?

____

____

____

____

____

____

What seems to be the Issue here?

____

____

____

____

What do I need to find out in the discussion with the Coachee in order to be of help to him or her?

Do I have a story from my experience that is related to this case and that I could (eventually) share with the Coachee?

Do I experience any additional thoughts or feelings?

YOUR NOTES:

12 PRACTICE CASE: PREPARING FOR A DIFFICULT CONVERSATION

Peter is a team leader in large technology-oriented multinational. He is 30, and he moved into this position slightly more than a year ago. He is doing well career-wise, and the company has recently put him through an internal assessment center, a mandatory step for those who aspire to be in the management talent pool. The nomination for the Assessment Center was a good signal for Peter. He believes he performed well during the assessment exercise. The most challenging part of the feedback he received was about his apparent unpreparedness for difficult conversations with employees, such as delivering bad news, disciplining people, demanding compliance when subordinates don't want to follow his requests, etc. When his boss, Arkadiy, read the report, he said to Peter: "You need to get tougher, you are too nice. You don't go far by being nice in this organization."

About six months ago Alex, a member of Peter's team, went on a paternal leave which was supposed to last for three months. Peter and HR managed to find a temporary replacement, Julia, who had been doing the job very much similar to Alex's about six years ago, but then left the workforce to take care of the family. She was now trying to get back to work. As someone who was out of the labor market for a considerable amount of time she didn't have too many options, but this temporary assignment could be a good way of relearning her skills and increasing her future chances. She knew that this was a three-month only opportunity, but was keen on taking it.

Alex then informed the company that he was prolonging his leave for another three months, as his spouse couldn't take hers due to her work considerations. Julia's contract was extended by another three months. By now she was functioning in an extremely efficient and productive manner, performing her tasks marvelously. Peter was happy to have Julia for another three months, and he felt that she was doing the job much better than Alex.

The department used a couple of interns who were helping the teams with their daily routines and some back-burner tasks that had been postponed in the past but now needed urgent completion. One of them was Tim, a 22-year old last year student at a local university. Arkadiy recently asked for a formal evaluation of the interns' performance, and Peter gladly provided positive comments about Tim's assistance with a couple of issues his team faced.

Peter received a message from Alex who informed him and HR that he was not planning to return to work from his parental leave. Apparently, his spouse just received a good placement on a different continent, and Alex would be moving with her and the kid there. To Peter it sounded like good news. He thought that he could keep Julia in Alex's place. When the news about Alex's departure became public, Peter caught Julia looking at him rather nervously: she was obviously thinking what Alex's departure could offer her in terms of a career opportunity. Peter gave her a big smile and saw her respond with what he classified as a big relief.

Peter sits with Arkadiy to talk about the personnel on his team. Arkadiy mentions that now that there is a vacancy in Peter's team, it can be filled by Tim, one of the interns whom everybody seems to like. Peter is trying to say that he already has a candidate, moreover, someone who thoroughly knows the job and has been on it for several months. Arkadiy is not impressed. For some reason he really wants Tim to be on the team. And, by the way, hasn't Peter given a high evaluation of Tim's contribution?

Peter tries to say that Julia probably expects that her temporary contract would turn into a permanent employment and that it would be very tough for him to disappoint her, given her high performance. He almost says to Arkadiy that he implicitly encouraged Julia to expect this appointment by giving her a big encouraging smile when Alex's departure was announced. The last moment he chooses not to do so, as that wouldn't fly well with Arkadiy. He just says that it would be difficult for him to disappoint Julia and to lose the high-performing worker and replace her with an inexperienced kid.

Arkadiy reminds him that as a team leader Peter has to bring Tim up to speed quickly. As far as disappointing Julia is concerned, he reminds

Peter about his developmental need to be effective in difficult conversation. He ends the meeting by saying: "Let's see how you have been developing in this direction, Peter."

CASE REFLECTION QUESTIONS:

What is my first reaction to the story presented?

What seems to be the Issue here?

What do I need to find out in the discussion with the Coachee in order to be of help to him or her?

Do I have a story from my experience that is related to this case and that I could (eventually) share with the Coachee?

Do I experience any additional thoughts or feelings?

YOUR NOTES:

13 PRACTICE CASE: LEARNING TO DELEGATE

Michael is 35. He has been working for ABC, his current employer, one of the global leaders in pharmaceuticals, since graduating from university eleven years ago. Currently Michael works in the M&A department where he heads a team of four people. The job of his team involves exploration of potential partnerships with or acquisitions of promising start-ups or academic spin-offs in the field of life sciences. There is a lot of analytics involved in the job, and there are always very tight deadlines, as competitors of ABC are often looking at the same partnership or acquisition targets. Decision-makers in his organization are utterly demanding, and Michael knows that they are very intolerant of sloppy work or mistakes.

Michael loves his job, and he loves the cognitive challenge of dealing with data, building models, and making projections. Sitting in front of the computer and playing with the numbers gives him an immense internal satisfaction. He is also very proud of the fact that his boss constantly makes it clear for Michael that he deeply appreciates his skills and job attitude.

The four people working for Michael are all clever and hard-working, although significantly less experienced than Michael. They are in their late twenties, and none has worked at ABC for more than two years. Michael likes his team, and he even spends time with them outside of working hours. They periodically go out together and have a lot of fun. "Work hard, play hard" has always been Michael's motto.

In a recent company-sponsored management development seminar Michael learned about the concept of "management styles" and completed a self-assessment exercise. As a result of this exercise, Michael associated his behavior with the style that is characterized by:

- taking personal responsibility for every important task the team faces,
- being ready to "roll-up" one's sleeves and do the job of his team-members when they are incapable or overstretched to do the job,
- trusting people with the tasks only after they have performed them under his direct supervision,
- double-checking the work given to others,
- being constantly on the run, and
- if the work that needs to be done by subordinates requires too much explanation and help on the part of the manager, choosing to do it himself.

While the instructor at the seminar explained the benefits and the risks associated with this style, Michael didn't really pay much attention to this part of the training. However, when a month later his company put him through a mandatory 360-degree feedback process and he received his feedback report, he vividly remembered the discussion at the course. His major "Area for Improvement" was clearly identified as "Delegation". He was scored very low on this dimension by both his subordinates, peers, and the boss.

In the qualitative commentaries section of the 360-degree report he could read the following commentaries left by his observers:

- Michael is a great analyst. He should now develop the skills of managing analysts.
- Michael is always on the run. He never explains what he wants from me. When he is unhappy with the result of my work, he simply does it himself.
- I sometimes feel that I can't use my skills because Michael wants to do the work himself.
- Michael should stop doing what he likes most (analysis) and concentrate on other aspects of the job, while leaving the analysis to his team.

Discussing the results of his 360-degree feedback with his boss over lunch, Michael realizes that the boss thinks that delegation skills is clearly an area of concern for Michael's professional future. At the same time, the boss makes it clear that the standards for the analytical work of Michael's team are very high, and that he should continue to deliver the highest quality work possible. Michael finds it difficult to reconcile the two demands: how can he delegate more while ensuring the quality that only he can deliver? He understands that if he wants to progress in his managerial responsibilities, he needs to delegate more. On the other hand, he is pretty sure that if the quality of the work drops down, he will be held personally responsible for it, and there may simply be no chances for managerial progress and upward career mobility.

CASE REFLECTION QUESTIONS:

What is my first reaction to the story presented?

____
____
____
____
____
____

What seems to be the Issue here?

____
____
____
____
____
____

What do I need to find out in the discussion with the Coachee in order to be of help to him or her?

____
____
____
____
____
____

Do I have a story from my experience that is related to this case and that I could (eventually) share with the Coachee?

____
____
____
____
____

Do I experience any additional thoughts or feelings?

____
____
____
____
____
____

YOUR NOTES:

14 PRACTICE CASE: AM I A QUOTA WOMAN?

Catherine is 32 years old. She is trained as an electronics engineer, and her specialization is rather rare. Her skills are in high demand by modern technology-driven organizations, and it looks like the demand will be growing in the future, as there are relatively few university programs that train people in this area. There are very few women in her field as well.

Catherine works as a project manager in a large global company with German roots. The company has recently announced that its priority is to attract more women to its predominantly male workforce, and to create conditions for growth for the number of women among its managers. Support of the career of female employees is widely publicized, and managers are expected to embrace this aspect of cultural change. Catherine fully enjoys the engineering aspects of her work, and she has quite cordial working relations with other people in her team, all of them male. Her bosses and colleagues fully respect her skills and expertise, and, despite being the only woman on the team, she has never had any of the issues she sometimes reads about in books and articles about women's challenges in the workforce.

Catherine's boss' boss, Theo, calls her to his office one day and informs her that Alejandro, the leader of the team to which she belongs and Catherine's direct superior, will be leaving making a move to another country. The position that becomes vacant is offered to Catherine, as Theo believes that she is well qualified and motivated to be a success in this role. Catherine is thrilled. Theo warns her, however, that some people might be a bit surprised by this choice, as there are several well qualified and experienced team members who could fit the job requirements. One of the critical tasks for Catherine is to maintain the morale in the team. It is also important that people want to stay with the company, as competition is getting aggressive in trying to target some of the specialists that are not readily available in the market.

When the news about Catherine's appointment is brought to the team by Theo, the response is lukewarm. People say a few congratulatory words to Catherine, but there is nothing more. Catherine understands that if some people expected to get her new job, they may need some time to deal with disappointment, but she doesn't understand why some of the younger members of the team, those who wouldn't be in competition for this job at all, also seem a bit cold and distant when the news is announced. She eventually shrugs it off, as there are lots of things to do for her and the team.

About two months into the new role, Catherine gets a call from Theo who requests an urgent meeting. It turns out that Marco, a 40-year-old team veteran and one of the most established experts, has submitted a resignation letter to HR. This came as a complete surprise to Theo, and now, obviously, to Catherine. Catherine immediately felt betrayed: why didn't Marco even talk to her? Theo asks if Catherine knows what is going on, and when she has no answer, he reminds her that he expects her to manage the stability of the team.

When Catherine is back from Theo's office she requests a conversation with Marco by sending him an email. The latter responds that he is busy, and that he needs the time to finish some of the important things, as before leaving the company he plans to go on a long vacation that he has accumulated.

Catherine has to leave for an important business trip to see an annoying customer and handle a few important issues with malfunctioning equipment. When she returns, she finds out that Marco has had an exit interview with HR, and that his decision to leave was prompted by Catherine's appointment as a team leader, a move that he considered to be purely driven by the company's "fad of the day": the women's diversity program. The HR contact said that Marco uttered the words: "I simply don't want to work for a quota woman." These words hurt Catherine a lot.

Nowhere in the discussions with Theo, in presentation of her appointment to the team, or in any of the conversations with other managers in the company has the issue of gender quotas ever come up. Catherine has always felt that it was her hard work and motivation that brought her to this position. But now she wonders if Theo has in fact promoted her to meet the quota requirements. She is also wondering about the attitude of her all-male team-members.

CASE REFLECTION QUESTIONS:

What is my first reaction to the story presented?

What seems to be the Issue here?

What do I need to find out in the discussion with the Coachee in order to be of help to him or her?

Do I have a story from my experience that is related to this case and that I could (eventually) share with the Coachee?

Do I experience any additional thoughts or feelings?

YOUR NOTES:

15 PRACTICE CASE: DO I HAVE A CHANCE?

Gerhardt is a 44-year-old marketing manager in large global technology company with German roots. He has been following what he believes to be a somewhat traditional career path for his generation: a university degree in business administration that took him seven years to complete, followed by a Doctorate that took another four years, and then, at the age of 30, his first business job with the current employer. His career progress after that has been stable, although not particularly quick. Almost everybody around seemed to have a similar career experience. The job itself is comfortable and well-paid. It allows for a reasonable "work-life" balance and gives Gerhardt enough time to spend with his children who are six and eight, and leaves enough time for his hobbies: photography and gardening.

There have been a few recent changes in the organization where Gerhardt works. First and foremost, there was a change in the CEO. The old CEO retired, and the successor, rather unusually, was brought from outside. Newspapers discussed this move as the Supervisory Board's desire to bring fresh blood into the organization and shake up a bit the very conservative nature of Gerhardt's company. With the arrival of the new CEO there were a few changes at the executive management level. In particular, there were a new Senior VP (and Board Member) of Marketing, and a new Senior VP (and Board Member) of Human Resources.

Some of the early announcements made by the new people struck Gerhardt as potentially challenging. The new CEO said that the organization was relying too much on its German origin, which was reflected in the predominance of Germans in the management ranks despite the fact that the majority of the company's operations were taking place elsewhere in the world. It was also announced that the company wasn't living up to the demands and realities of today's world. In particular, it was dominated by male managers, even in areas where the labor market could supply quite a few talented female candidates. Last but not least, the new CEO made a statement that the managerial ranks of the organization were "brought up in old leadership paradigms", and that new, younger leaders were needed. Those statements relatively quickly translated in a number of initiatives in the organization. The company launched an aggressive diversity program. It was announced that, although the company was trying to embrace all possible aspects of diversity, for the time being it would concentrate on two aspects: women's participation in the management ranks, and giving chances to the new generation of managers. A cynical colleague of Gerhardt shared with him a joke, reflecting some of the attitudes towards such initiatives: "A forty-five year-old male was hired by our company. And he even made a career."

Gerhardt has just been approached by HR informing him that as part of the company's career development program he is invited to take part in a leadership assessment center exercise. Going through such an exercise and "passing" it successfully is a necessary prerequisite for moving anywhere higher of Gerhardt's current career level in the organization. Gerhardt truly hates all those exercises that he knows make part of an assessment center: making analysis of the data and then creating an artificial strategy presentation, solving a business case through a leaderless group discussion, imitating a conversation with a difficult employee played by an actor, going through an in-depth interview with a psychologist, etc. He truly questions the validity of the Assessment Center methodology in predicting success on the job, and he also feels utterly uncomfortable performing under observation.

At lunch Gerhardt meets Paul, an old-time acquaintance from a different division of his company whom Gerhardt first met during his university times. Paul tells him about his recent experience in an Assessment Center, and shares some of the tasks he had to complete. Semi-jokingly Paul adds that he has realized that never before he had an experience of discussing a business case in a group where half of the participants were women. That was quite a new thing for him. He ends his story by saying: "The most unusual thing was being the oldest person in the group. The rest of the people were much younger, some of them probably below thirty."

Reflecting on this conversation and his own forthcoming Assessment

Center, Gerhardt contemplates if it makes any sense for him to go through the painful exercise. Does he really have a chance in the current company situation where he clearly doesn't belong to the employee categories in which the organization seeks its managerial talent? Does he want to play a "filler" role in the exercise and, potentially, become a piece of evidence that German males in their mid-forties are blocking the road for talented younger women and men who are much more equipped to lead this organization in the future? Should he find an excuse and turn down the invitation to participate in the Assessment Center?

CASE REFLECTION QUESTIONS:

What is my first reaction to the story presented?

What seems to be the Issue here?

What do I need to find out in the discussion with the Coachee in order to be of help to him or her?

Do I have a story from my experience that is related to this case and that I could (eventually) share with the Coachee?

____
____
____

Do I experience any additional thoughts or feelings?

____
____
____
____
____
____

YOUR NOTES:

16 PRACTICE CASE: ADVICE BEFORE MOVING TO THE WEST

Zhentang is a 26-year-old Chinese engineer working for a global company with significant presence and large future plans in Asia. She was recruited four years ago through a graduate recruitment program that the company used to canvass the leading Chinese universities in an attempt to bring desperately needed talent that the growth plans required. Zhentang went through a rigorous "boot camp" (as the internal six-months long training program was called) and then found her place in a team working on customization of the company's leading technology to the local needs of the Chinese market.

Four years after recruitment, she was one of few people from her cohort that were still with the company: the rest of the people had already switched jobs in the highly mobile labor market. The learning curve was pretty steep, and the opportunities for Chinese engineers with even minimal experience in global companies were plentiful. By local standards, Zhentang was perceived to be utterly loyal to her company.

In an attempt to retain talented and loyal employees, and recognizing the importance of Asia in general and China in particular for the future of the company, a program was designed to bring high potential young managers from China to other countries in order to expose them to different cultures and socialize them into the ways work is organized in other parts of the world. Those two year assignments should also serve as a training ground allowing the participants to get ready for higher levels of responsibility back in China.

While some of the assignments were with the French or US operations of the company, the majority of the participants went to Germany. Most of the assignments in the past were deemed to be very successful, with most delegates later returning to China and successfully assuming higher levels managerial positions. Some participants would remain in Europe where they would be offered an interesting position at the headquarters, and, in a few cases, the destination after the two-year expatriate stint would be another expatriate assignment, for example, in the Middle East or Africa.

A few of the assignments failed, finishing prematurely and leading to an early return of the delegate or even his or her departure from the company. The HR people usually say that the delegate's inability to adjust to the culture and Western management style is the major reason for failure.

Zhentang is interested in making her assignment a success. Her parents are very proud of her achievement at this young age, and their daughter's international assignment makes them happy. Zhentang thinks that this is a good timing for her, as her parents are still young enough and don't need her support for the next couple of years. She would be happy to come back to China after the assignment and continue her career there, being not too far away from her parents.

Zhentang wants to know what her Western colleagues expect of her as a as a subordinate, peer, and boss. She also wants to integrate well into the social fabric of the organization, as, as she knows, personal connections are very important in making things work inside the organization. She wants the time spent in the West be not only a learning opportunity, but also a foundation of the social ties that will be valued for the future. In addition, she wants the assignment to be an important part of her life experience. She has heard about colleagues who never ventured beyond their offices or production facilities while in Europe. For Zhentang it is important to have a life, and, hopefully, an enjoyable one.

Zhentang has heard about a few cases of the program participants' failure to adjust to the different working environment in Germany, France, or the United States. She has talked to HR about this issue, and they reassured her that they would send her to a cultural differences training course before the start of her assignment. However, following advice of some of her friends, she has decided to ask someone familiar with that environment for advice about how to find her way there and make the best out of her experience.

You name came to her mind as she went through a participant's booklet from a leadership conference that her company held several months ago and in which both of you participated. You happen to be going to China for a business trip, and Zhentang is ready to invite you to lunch so that she can talk to you.

CASE REFLECTION QUESTIONS:

What is my first reaction to the story presented?

What seems to be the Issue here?

What do I need to find out in the discussion with the Coachee in order to be of help to him or her?

Do I have a story from my experience that is related to this case and that I could (eventually) share with the Coachee?

Do I experience any additional thoughts or feelings?

YOUR NOTES:

17 PRACTICE CASE: BAD PRESENTATIONS, BAD 360-DEGREE FEEDBACK

Kevin is 31years old, and he works for a large global consulting company as a senior manager. As typical in the consulting world, he has to juggle a multitude of projects and clients at the same time. His situation is a bit complicated by the fact that he has to work closely with three different partners, all of them located in different cities across the country. Each of the three partners considers Kevin to be "his" senior manager, and, as a result, Kevin often gets conflicting requests and deadlines from them.

So far he has managed to juggle those requests (and egos) quite well, but often at the cost of his own time, sleep, and energy. Kevin also always overstretches his teams and he is aware that many junior consultants dread working for him. Kevin is very demanding but has very little time to spend with the team members to explain what they need to do. When they make a mistake, he doesn't hesitate to show his frustration. Kevin has been frequently reminded by each of the partners that people often complain about his way of treating subordinates. They all seem to think that this is Kevin's weakness (and none of them has ever acknowledged the challenge of Kevin's situation).

While working recently on two concurrent and urgent projects (supervised by two different partners), Kevin realized that he had too much on his shoulders. The goals of both projects were unreasonable, the managers on the clients' sides were totally uncooperative (and, in Kevin's deeply held opinion, utterly stupid), and the team members assigned to his projects were, in Kevin's mind, simply lazy. To make things worse, presentations of interim results to both clients were scheduled for the same day in two different cities: one in the early morning, the other in the late afternoon. This overlap was primarily caused by the partner availability and the client's urgency (a typical scenario in the anticipation of Easter vacations when everyone seemed to in a rush to get as much stuff "ticked off" so that they could completely forget about business for two weeks).

During the first presentation everything went wrong from the very first moment. First, a bulb in the client's computer projector burned and they had to wait for a replacement. Then the client started challenging the assumptions presented in the calculations used by Kevin's team. One of the clients' managers kept bugging Kevin about the numbers, and even found inconsistencies in a number of tables projected. Reluctantly, Kevin acknowledged some of the questionability of the figures in the charts (he was already mentally "killing" the associate who had prepared the tables while vaguely remembering the latter mentioning that the data supplied by the client didn't make much sense and him, Kevin, dismissing the issue).

The partner in charge of the project felt it necessary to intervene, make a few unreasonable promises to the client, and give an angry look to Kevin. The latter didn't have a chance to explain, as he had to rush to the airport to catch a plane for his next destination. The partner was livid.

The afternoon presentation was slightly better, but not without challenges either. Kevin was quite abrasive with the client's representatives, failed to let them finish their comments by jumping with his responses in the middle of their sentences, and dismissing the concerns expressed by the audience. The partner in charge of this project eventually took over. After the presentation, the partner asked Kevin what was going on, and what had happened to his basic consulting skills. Kevin mumbled something in response before catching a cab to go to the airport.

Checking his emails while waiting for the plain with a beer in a frequent flyer lounge, Kevin saw a message from HR with the 360-degree feedback (another of the stupid HR initiatives, thought Kevin) report attached to it. Kevin didn't expect much of a positive feedback from the team members working for him. However, he was shocked to see that the three partners also rated him pretty low on most of the dimensions used in the assessment. The two difficult presentations and now this report made Kevin feel like he was losing it. He was angry, frustrated, and scared at the same time. He desperately needed to talk to someone.

CASE REFLECTION QUESTIONS:

What is my first reaction to the story presented?

What seems to be the Issue here?

What do I need to find out in the discussion with the Coachee in order to be of help to him or her?

Do I have a story from my experience that is related to this case and that I could (eventually) share with the Coachee?

Do I experience any additional thoughts or feelings?

YOUR NOTES:

18 PRACTICE CASE: SHOULD I ASK FOR MORE REWARDS?

Marushka is a 31- year- old internal audit manager at XYZ, a large global company. Her job involves planning and executing internal audit projects at various parts of her organization, managing a team of six employees, and, in addition, liaising with the Internal Audit training manager in designing and developing training courses for the function. When Marushka joined XYZ about a year ago from the auditing arm of a global Big 4 auditing/consulting company, she did it primarily out of hope that at some point she would be able to leave audit-related jobs and develop herself for a position that would not be so much travel demanding.

At the time of entering XYZ, she was very excited by the opportunity, and she found the working conditions to be much better than at her previous employment place, as, although there was still a lot of travel, she could have more control in planning business trips and other aspects of her work. Having worked in a Big 4 company, Marushka received proper training and experience in training others, and she always considered training to be an important role in any manager's job. Although at times this training activity demanded a lot of extra effort and dedication that many of her colleagues never wanted to give, Marushka liked the training aspect of her work, as it allowed her to have some travel-free time when she would be preparing and delivering training courses in her home office. Marushka didn't negotiate the salary, as what she had been offered was 15% more than her compensation at her former Big 4 firm, and that was quite all right at that time.

While working on a recent project to which she had been assigned unexpectedly due to an injury suffered by the manager responsible for it,

Marushka accidentally bumped into a document containing salary data of some of her peers. While there was a professional need to look at the data in order to verify some calculations, Marushka also found something interesting about herself: she was significantly underpaid compared to the people at the same level (and in some cases, with the same less-than-a-year tenure in her company). The difference could be as high as twenty percent in a number of cases. Marushka had never thought about her salary as being unfair, but when she saw the data about some of her colleagues' earnings, she had a feeling of deep disappointment.

She felt even more disappointed when in some further files she found information about the costs of external training that some of her colleagues were receiving. A couple of people got training for a US Certified Public Accountant qualification, although they were Europeans based in Europe, and a couple of people were pursuing an Executive MBA at the company's cost. While Marushka had never considered further education for herself, she now realized that an Executive MBA could be a pretty good enhancer on the way out of Internal Audit and into some other functions in the organization.

By nature of her job and access to company data, Marushka knows that in her organization annual salary increases tend to be around 3-4%. She suspects that this is exactly what she is going to get as a result of this year's work. She is thinking if she should ask for a more significant increase now that she knows that she is significantly underpaid compared to a peer group, of if she should ask for a training opportunity, such as an Executive MBA. While asking for a raise might make her reveal the source of her information being work-related access to salary data files, she feels a bit uneasy about this, as some ethical questions pop up in her mind. Asking for an EMBA might be difficult, as she has only been in this company for a year, and Marushka is not sure if this would be enough to justify a request for such an investment. Marushka's annual review with her boss will take place in three weeks from today.

CASE REFLECTION QUESTIONS:

What is my first reaction to the story presented?

____

____

____

____

____

____

What seems to be the Issue here?

What do I need to find out in the discussion with the Coachee in order to be of help to him or her?

Do I have a story from my experience that is related to this case and that I could (eventually) share with the Coachee?

Do I experience any additional thoughts or feelings?

YOUR NOTES:

19 PRACTICE CASE: IT'S JUST TOO MUCH

Greg is 47. He is head of marketing analysis and planning for a large industrial engineering company. He has been on the job for quite some time to know it inside out. However, with the arrival of the new CEO, a former marketing executive himself, and a holder of a PhD in marketing with a dissertation on use of marketing analytics, Gregg feels that his function started getting unusual attention from the Senior VP of Marketing, and, at times, from the CEO himself.

People have started questioning some of the ways Greg's department has been doing its job, particularly some of the models used for projections of future demand. Greg's people have to spend a lot of time writing large methodology supplements to their reports and presentations, as, it seems, it becomes a company's sport to challenge them on the methods used. Greg feels that this may be the new CEO's old identity of a marketing researcher kicking in, and other people use it to attack Greg's department. Greg feels that when the methodology questions arise, his team's and his own professionalism are severely questioned. For the first time in the past several years he has started asking himself questions about his own job security.

However, the job is not the only challenge Greg has to deal with right now. His father to whom Greg was very close died a month ago, and now he needs to deal with the issue of his elderly mother's deteriorating health and inability to live independently. She is in the early stages of Alzheimer's, and the disease is progressing. When Greg's father was alive, it wasn't a big deal for Greg, as the father could manage the couple's daily life, but now it has become pretty obvious that Greg's mother needed assistance on a daily basis. While the mother lives only 300 kilometers away from Greg's home, it is not possible to go there every day and help her. Greg is considering a number of options, including an assisted living (a nursing home) arrangement for his mother, hiring external care (which would go beyond what the elderly care insurance would cover), or bringing his mother to live with Greg and his family. The first two options would be a financial stretch. The last option is something that Greg's wife, who has never been particularly fond of Greg's mother, is not supporting. Her arguments are that their house is small, and that Greg is always busy, and she doesn't feel qualified to add nursing duties to her daily job and responsibilities for two teenagers who are not easy to deal with.

And those teenagers are another set of worries for Greg. One of them, a 10th grader, is deeply in love and refuses to pay attention to anyone or anything beyond her boyfriend who is currently struggling with his apprenticeship as a baker. The other, a 9th grader, spends all of his free time on building an athletic figure and increasing his muscle mass. Both seem to ignore the parents' attempts to influence their lives.

In addition, there are a couple of painful things that need to be done with the house. The gas heater needs replacement, and so does some of the plumbing and roofing on the house. Greg acknowledges that he has been postponing some of the issues for far too long, and those home improvements can't wait any longer.

All those things taken together make Greg feel overwhelmed. To make things worse, Greg's best employee, the one who is the most qualified to handle the methodology questions coming from the CEO, has just announced his resignation. "It's just too much. I simply can't handle this any longer," says Gregg.

CASE REFLECTION QUESTIONS:

What is my first reaction to the story presented?

____

____

____

____

____

____

What seems to be the Issue here?

____
____
____
____
____
____

What do I need to find out in the discussion with the Coachee in order to be of help to him or her?

____
____
____
____
____
____

Do I have a story from my experience that is related to this case and that I could (eventually) share with the Coachee?

____
____
____
____
____
____

Do I experience any additional thoughts or feelings?

____
____
____
____
____
____

YOUR NOTES:

20 PRACTICE CASE: DO I LIVE UP TO MY VALUES?

Victor is a 44-years-old Russian senior manager working for a global company. He perceives himself to be a person who shares Western values, in particular, respect for an individual. He openly underscores the importance of those values in his professional work, and he wants to transmit them to his employees, as well as to his three children, who are six, eight, and eleven years of age. A recent incident at a large all-inclusive vacation resort in the South of Spain where Victor and his family were spending their vacation made him, however, question the extent to which he really ascribed to and lived up to his proclaimed values. This is how Victor describes the situation.

"On the last day of our nice vacation we booked a table at one of the best restaurants in the resort complex where we were vacationing. This restaurant is very popular with the vacationers, as it makes part of the all-inclusive arrangement while offering a sit-down menu service. Besides, it is located exactly on the sea-shore, so guests can enjoy beautiful sunsets and pleasant sea wind. All that coupled with the casual and child-friendly atmosphere made this restaurant a great place for dinner. We had been there before with my wife, and for the last evening of our vacation we brought our children with us.

As the place is very popular, the tables are placed rather close to one another, at times making it uncomfortable for the people sitting at them, as you can easily disturb people at another table when you move your chair or stand up. I quickly realized that people sitting at a table next to ours were the ones whom we had sat next to during our previous dinner at this restaurant. It was a couple with two children, one about fourteen, and the other about nineteen. The people were rather heavily-bodied, and I could vividly remember the discomfort felt when we were trying to "negotiate" physically our space around our respective tables the last time. This time two of our smaller kids were sitting on the side that was neighboring that family's table, so there seemed to be enough of space.

With the service being quite lengthy, allowing people to enjoy the evening, my kids started getting a bit bored, and, after making a few games with one another, started moving around the restaurant, going to the beach adjacent to the restaurant, the self-service juice bar, restrooms, etc. Apparently, they disturbed the other family, while trying to get out of the narrow aisle between the tables, currently occupied to a large extent by the chairs of the other family. At some point, the young man, the one who looked nineteen, turned to my children, addressed them directly, and reprimanded them for constant moving around. I explained to my kids that they should be more careful when moving and said that in such instances they should say "Excuse me, please". The young man seemed to be satisfied. However, a bit later, the children were moving again, and, apparently, disturbing the people at the other table.

The young man turned to us and made what I considered to be an unhappy grimace. My wife suggested that since the aisle between the tables was rather narrow, maybe the young man could be more comfortable sitting at another free chair at his table, and then he wouldn't be disturbed by the kids moving around. At this moment the woman from the other table stood up, making her way out, and said: "You don't get it. The main problem is the noise that your children are making. They are so noisy." Well, that wasn't the quietest possible restaurant. There was a baby crying, and many other kids running around, which was totally understandable at a family resort. For some reason, however, that statement made me extremely angry.

I told the woman that my children were free people in a free country, and that the family resort concept usually means that there are children and their noise everywhere. Then, addressing the young man who was still smirking, I said that it is really ridiculous when overweight people make an issue with kids bothering them in a narrow aisle between the dinner tables. My wife was trying to tell me to shut up. The woman and the young man were silent, but gave me a somewhat disbelieving look. Then they left. The young man and teenage girl remained at their table, but a bit later, without waiting for their deserts, they stood up and left as well, the man saying "Have a good evening" to us on his way out."

The situation made Victor feel ill at ease. He realized that he has done something inappropriate, something that was in deep contradiction with his values and the view he wanted to have of himself. He was ashamed for his behavior, and thought that he wasn't the best possible role model for his own children. He also thought that he spoiled the evening for his wife, as well as the other family.

He made several attempts to rationalize his behavior. For example, Victor made it vivid in his memory how during the previous dinner at the same restaurant he had said nothing when the young man had moved some parts of his large body very close to the heads of Victor and his wife while making his way to the table. He also tried to convince himself that his remark wasn't too bad, as he didn't use the word "fat" (which was almost at the tip of his tongue and only at the last moment was substituted for "overweight"). Still, he quickly realized his attempts at rationalizations, and he couldn't stop questioning his own nature as a human being. He spent sleepless night thinking about what this incident could mean for his view of himself, his behavior, and his worth as a parent and a manager. He was also wondering if he would be able to handle his frustrations more productively in the future.

CASE REFLECTION QUESTIONS:

What is my first reaction to the story presented?

What seems to be the Issue here?

What do I need to find out in the discussion with the Coachee in order to be of help to him or her?

Do I have a story from my experience that is related to this case and that I could (eventually) share with the Coachee?

Do I experience any additional thoughts or feelings?

YOUR NOTES:

21 PRACTICE CASE: FOLLOWING UP ON AN ACTION PLAN

Carlos is a 39-year-old manager in a large fast moving consumer goods company. As part of the company's leadership development approach, he recently took part in a number of courses offered by various business schools and covering a range of topics, such as Finance, Strategy, Innovation, Consumer Behavior, etc. One of the modules taken in a leading European business school was dedicated to the topic of leadership. The five-day long leadership program, in addition to a variety of workshops, case-studies, and simulations, included a 360-degree feedback process (completed prior to the session) and a subsequent one day group coaching session. The group coaching session, although based on the results of the 360-degree feedback, went, to Carlos' surprise, beyond the results of this specific assessment and concentrated on a broader set of issues of leadership philosophy, career aspirations, and overall life satisfaction. Carlos was really astonished at how quickly people opened up and engaged in discussion of deep personal issues.

At the end of the session, Carlos and other participants were asked to select one or two issues that had come up during the coaching day, and that they were willing to work on as a result of the course. Participants were asked to record those aspects in a document called "A Letter to Myself". This letter would be put in a self-addressed envelope, sealed, and then submitted to the program manager. The latter would send the letter to the participants to remind them of their own commitments approximately six weeks after the course. Participants were also encouraged to agree with another member of the class to act as mutual peer coaches and to set up a phone conversation to discuss each other's progress with implementations of the action ideas developed during the seminar.

The issue identified by Carlos as something that was important for him to work on had to do with increasing his visibility in the organization. During the coaching session it became pretty clear that Carlos was undermining his team's efforts by not developing enough of visibility and support with other departments and functions of his organization. As a result, his people experienced difficulties getting help and information from other functions of the organization. Carlos' own career could potentially be in jeopardy, as his organization tried to promote networking among managers and employees and encouraged informal problem-solving. Carlos recognized that this was very different from his previous employment experience with large technology organizations where problems would be normally solved by way of escalating to the top managers. The experience of a networked organization was something new to him.

The action steps identified by Carlos included reaching out to peers in his organization by inviting them to lunch, asking people to attend his own team meetings and asking to attend team meetings organized by peers, and, possibly, engaging in a cross-functional project. When Carlos identified those action steps in the context of a group coaching session, they all sounded quite reasonable and doable. However, back at work, he got quickly sucked into the routine of daily tasks and problems. He once tried to send an email to a peer of his inviting her to have lunch and talk about improving communication between their teams, but she politely rejected all of the three dates offered by Carlos mentioning a time clash with her in-company yoga classes and not offering an alternative.

After this uncomfortable attempt bringing no result, Carlos didn't try anything else. He was pretty busy, and that was enough of an excuse not to put himself in a situation where he would feel uncomfortable again. While from time to time he was reminding himself about the commitments made at the leadership course, he could always rationalize why he couldn't act on those. With the time passing and the course remaining further away in the past, it became easier and easier to do so.

This morning a letter arrived in the post. Carlos recognized his own handwriting on the envelope. He knew immediately what was inside. To make matters worse, a reminder from his Outlook calendar popped up: "Schedule a follow-up peer coaching conversation to discuss the Action Plan from the Leadership course."

CASE REFLECTION QUESTIONS:

What is my first reaction to the story presented?

What seems to be the Issue here?

What do I need to find out in the discussion with the Coachee in order to be of help to him or her?

Do I have a story from my experience that is related to this case and that I could (eventually) share with the Coachee?

Do I experience any additional thoughts or feelings?

YOUR NOTES:

22 JUMP STARTING A COACHING SESSION IN A COACHEE ROLE

Making the most out of a peer coaching session in the role of a Coachee requires some effort. At the end of the day, peer coaching is a mutual learning opportunity with mutual responsibilities for a successful outcome of a meaningful conversation.

If you are taking part in a peer coaching exercise in an executive education program and you haven't been asked to prepare for a coaching session in advance, take a couple of moments to think about what you are going to explore as part of your experience. Think about an Issue that is important for you professionally (or, if you wish, personally).

The Issue (opportunity, challenge, task, hope, problem, relationship, action item, etc.) that I would like to explore is:

Identify and communicate the expectations from the session. Inform the Peer Coach if you want feedback on your plan/style/ideas, etc. If your objective is to have a sparring partner for a discussion of ideas, let your coaching partner know. If you need to tap into the specific expertise of the Peer Coach in an area important for your successful implementation of the plan or ideas, tell this to the Peer Coach. However, don't be disappointed if the other party for some reason is not willing/capable of helping you with such a request directly.

This is what I want to get from the Peer Coach in this exercise:

Prepare your own story regarding the issue you want to raise with the peer coach. For example, be ready to explain why a particular item on your action plan is really important. Treat your story as a draft. Use this as a learning opportunity for exploring the relationship between you and your Issue.

This is what I think I want to learn about myself and my relationship with my Issue:

YOUR NOTES:

23 PREPARING FOR YOUR PEER COACHING SESSION IN ADVANCE

If you have an opportunity to prepare for your peer coaching session in advance, please use the following approach to structure your thinking and your story in order to make the best use of your peer coaching opportunity. This structure can be used to prepare for individual or group peer coaching sessions.

Think about a key Issue that you are facing. This can be related to opportunities (e.g. an offer to participate in a new project at work), fantasies (e.g. accelerating your career progress while maintaining your life style), hopes (e.g. changing your professional field as a result of your additional education), fears (e.g. starting in a completely new role with unclear tasks), relationships (e.g. gaining trust with a new boss), or anything that is important to you.

Ideally, the Issue that can be productively discussed in a peer coaching session should meet a few criteria. These criteria are adapted from the work of Ron Heifetz and Marty Linsky from the Kennedy School of Governance at Harvard University as presented in their "Art and Practice of Leadership Development" seminar:

- You should be willing to get help with that Issue, and that means that you should be willing to discuss it in the context of a peer coaching session (individual and/or group).

- This Issue should be expected to have a serious impact on your performance or success (professionally or personally) and/or serious impact on the effectiveness of your organization or a part of it.

- This Issue should be expected to have an impact on other individuals (in your personal or professional life).
- You should be truly open to explore the Issue, to consider alternative possibilities, and to hear challenging questions related to your relationship with the Issue.

Prepare a description of your Issue here. You can also use a separate sheet, making sure that it is no longer than one page.

Describe the Issue you are facing from your perspective. The Issue (opportunity, challenge, task, hope, problem, relationship, action item, etc.) that I would like to explore is:

____

____

____

____

____

____

____

____

____

____

Identify the major stakeholders (other individuals) who are affected by your Issue or the way you handle it. Identify their major interests. You may want to disguise the real names of the people.

____

____

____

____

____

____

____

____

____

____

Describe the actions you have taken or you plan to take with regard to your Issue. How the stakeholders have been affected or will be affected by your actions? What has been or would be their reaction? How does that influence your relationship with your Issue?

Can you think of a question that you could pose to yourself and your Peer Coach that can help start the conversation during your peer coaching session?

YOUR NOTES:

24 ACTION PLAN

Upon a completion of a peer coaching session you should have an idea about an action plan for you to work on as a result of your joint learning experience with you Peer Coach or peer coaching group.

As a tangible result of the peer coaching interaction, you may develop a personal letter of commitment. Discuss it with a peer coach, and make a copy for her or him. Agree on the follow-up discussion to see how you are doing in terms of fulfilling your personal obligations. In some programs you will be offered an opportunity to have a sealed copy of your letter sent to you by program staff. A possible template for a letter of commitment is provided on the next pages.

When thinking about an action plan, make sure that you make a reasonable and manageable commitment. It is better to start in a small, experiential mode and then expand based on the results of your experimentation.

YOUR NOTES:

A Letter to Myself

I had a peer coaching session on ______________________________(date)
at____(place).

The main learning points from my peer coaching sessions are:

____
____
____
____
____
____
____

My next steps based on those learning points will be:

____
____
____
____
____
____
____

What will help me start/maintain the changes I am planning to make/I have made?

____
____
____
____
____
____
____

How will I remind myself to continue working on my growth and progress?

____
____
____
____
____
____
____

What aspects may be the most challenging for me?

____

Whom do I need to ask for help/support or whose help/support do I need to be willing to accept?

____

What resources would be most valuable to me?

____

Additional notes:

____

Date for planned follow-up with a peer coach

____

Signature ____

25 YOUR PERSONAL CHAPTER

This is your personal chapter in this publication. Please use the space provided to reflect on your interest in practicing peer coaching as a Coachee and Peer Coach. If you are taking part in an executive course, take notes related to the course content here. Jot down lessons learned and ideas developed. Take note about things to look up further or people to contact later. In short, create your own chapter in the *Peer Coaching Practice for Managers* book.

YOUR NOTES:

YOUR NOTES:

YOUR NOTES:

YOUR NOTES:

YOUR NOTES:

26 REFERENCES

Allamby, D. *The Manager's Coaching Toolkit*, Harlow: Pearson Education.

Arnold, R., & Pätzold, H. (2007). *Schulpädagogik kompakt.* Berlin: Cornelsen-Scriptor.

Coren, A. (1997). *A Psychodynamic Approach to Education.* London: Sheldon Press.

Kets de Vries, M.F.R. (2011). *The Hedgehog Effect: Executive Coaching and The Secrets of Building High Performance Teams.* San Francisco: Jossey-Bass.

Kets de Vries, M.F.R.., Korotov, K., & Florent-Treacy, E. (2007). *Coach and Couch: The Psychology of Making Better Leaders.* Houndmills and New York: Palgrave.

Kets de Vries, M.F.R., Guillen, L., Korotov, K., & Florent-Treacy, E. (2010). *The Coaching Kaleidoscope: Insights from the Inside.* Houndmills and New York: Palgrave.

Korotov, K.. (2008). Peer Coaching in Executive Education Programs. *Training and Management Development Methods*, 22 (2): 3.15 – 3.24.

Korotov, K., Florent-Treacy, E., Kets de Vries, M.F.R., & Bernhardt, A. (2012). *Tricky Coaching: Difficult Cases in Leadership Coaching.* Houndmills and New York: Palgrave.

Landsberg, M.(1997). *The Tao of Coaching.* London: HarperCollinsBusiness

Pätzold, H. (2011). *Learning and Teaching in Adult Education: Contemporary Theories*. Opladen & Farmington Hills, MI: Barbara Budrich Publishers.

Rehr, M., & Gruber, H. (2007). Netzwerkanalyse in der Pädagogik. *Zeitschrift für Pädagogik*, 53 (2): 243-264.

Whitmore, J. (2002). *Coaching for Performance*, 3rd. Ed. London: Nicholas Brealey

ABOUT THE AUTHOR

Professor Konstantin Korotov, PhD conducts research and teaches at the ESMT – European School of Management and Technology in Berlin, Germany. His interests are leadership development, executive coaching, and executive education. He teaches in the MBA and Executive MBA programs, and in the Leading People and Teams and Leading with Psychological Intelligence open enrollment executive education programs. He has taught in corporate executive programs for, among others, Deutsche Bank, Lufthansa, E.ON, RWE, EnBW, Ernst & Young, KPMG, Deloitte, Xerox, Rosatom, Russian Railroads, Elster Group, Allianz, Daimler, McDonald's, Johnson & Johnson, Deutsche Telekom, Qatar Telecom, Hyatt International, Axel Springer, etc.
He can be contacted at konstantin.korotov@esmt.org

21199491R00055

Made in the USA
Charleston, SC
11 August 2013